HOUSEHOLD INVENTIONS

FROM TOILETS TO TOASTERS

by Natalie Lunis

Consultant: Paul F. Johnston, Washington, D.C.

BEARPORT
PUBLISHING COMPANY, INC.

New York, New York

Credits:
Cover and title page, Michelle Barbera (illustrator), Rafal Zdeb/istockphoto (lightbulb), Mark Evans/ istockphoto (alarm clock); 4, Archivo Iconografico, S.A./CORBIS; 5(t), Christopher Anderson/ Spokane Spokesman Rev/WpN; 6, Bettmann/Corbis; 7(b), CORBIS; 8, Historical Picture Archive/ CORBIS; 9(t), CORBIS; 9(b), CORBIS; 11(t), Joop Greypink/Stone/Getty Images; 11(b), Hemera Technologies/Alamy; 12, Buzz Pictures/Alamy; 13(t), Reuters/CORBIS; 13(b), Douglas McFadd/ Getty Images; 14, Bettmann/CORBIS; 15(t), Araldo de Luca/CORBIS; 15(b), Réunion des Musées Nationaux /Art Resource, NY; 16(l), Archivo Iconografico, S.A./CORBIS; 16(r), Mike Booth/ Alamy; 17(t), Michael Pohuski/FoodPix/GettyImages; 17(b), Tim Flach/Stone/Getty Images; 19(t), Steve Wisbauer/Index Stock Imagery/PictureQuest; 19(b), Ann Stratton/Foodpix; 20, James L. Amos/CORBIS; 21(t), Comstock Images/Alamy; 22, John Jenkins, www.sparkmuseum.com; 23(b), Alan Schein Photography/CORBIS; 24, Howard Kingsnorth/Taxi/GettyImages; 25(t),T. Hoenig/A. B./zefa/Corbis; 25(b), MIT Media Lab.

Design and production by Dawn Beard Creative and Octavo Design and Production, Inc.

Library of Congress Cataloging-in-Publication Data

Lunis, Natalie.
  Household inventions : from toilets to toasters / by Natalie Lunis.
    p. cm. — (Which came first?)
  Includes bibliographical references and index.
  ISBN 1-59716-131-4 (library binding) — ISBN 1-59716-138-1 (pbk.)
  1. Inventions—History—Juvenile literature. 2. Household appliances—United States—History— Juvenile literature. I. Title. II. Series.

T15.L86 2006
609—dc22
                    2005029612

For more information, write to Bearport Publishing Company, Inc., 101 Fifth Avenue, Suite 6R, New York, New York 10003. Printed in the United States of America.

1 2 3 4 5 6 7 8 9 10

Contents

7

11

17

21

23

Introduction

Life in the old days wasn't easy. About 200 years ago, many people had to boil clothes to clean them. Going to the "bathroom" often meant going outside to a little shack, even in the coldest weather.

Today people are lucky. The washing machine, toilet, and lots of other household inventions have made a big difference. Life at home is safer, cleaner, and a lot more comfortable.

This book describes ten pairs of household inventions. Read about each pair and guess which one came first. Then turn the page for the answer.

▲ **Many people washed their clothes in a stream before the washing machine was invented. Some people still wash their clothes this way today.**

Turn the page to
find out which
came first.

Which Came First?

Air Conditioner

People used electric fans before they had air conditioners. Fans can make a breeze, but they can't cool the air. So homes were still hot.

▲ In a recent survey, the air conditioner was voted the "best idea" from a list of important American inventions.

▲ More U.S. households own and use refrigerators than any other appliance. In fact, refrigerators are found in 99.5 percent of American homes.

Refrigerator

Before there were electric refrigerators, people used iceboxes to keep food cool in their homes. An icebox was a large wooden box that held food in one section and a large block of ice in another.

5

Answer: Refrigerator

The first modern household refrigerators were developed and sold between 1913 and 1927. The first household air conditioners went on the market in 1929. Both devices were used by businesses before they became household **appliances**. Refrigerators were used in food-processing plants and grocery stores. Air conditioners cooled off factories, department stores, and movie theaters.

▲ **Early wooden refrigerator, around 1921**

The earliest refrigerators were made of wood. Metal refrigerators were introduced in the mid-1920s.

Turn the page to find out which came first.

Which Came First?

Shower

The modern shower depends on indoor **plumbing**. One set of pipes in the house brings in clean water. Another set carries away used, dirty water.

Toilet

Modern toilets also require plumbing to work. Before homes had the necessary water pipes, many people used outdoor toilets in shacks. These little buildings were called "outhouses."

▲ **In 1935, each of these houses in Cincinnati, Ohio, had an outhouse in the backyard where people went to the bathroom.**

7

Answer: Toilet

Today's toilet was developed in England over a 100-year period beginning in 1775. For most of that time, Americans **imported** English-made toilets. American companies finally began making them in the late 1800s.

Most Americans took baths instead of showers until the early 1900s. That's the time when the first bathtubs with built-in showers were sold.

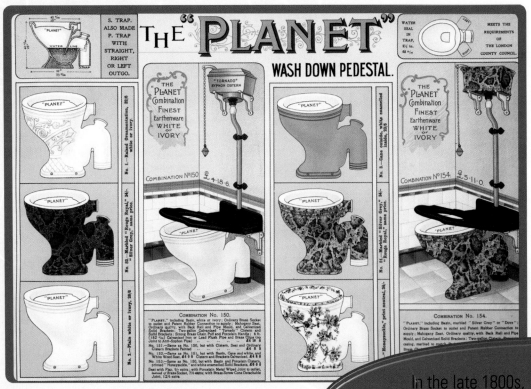

In the late 1800s, English companies made fancy toilets with painted designs. Some were even shaped like dolphins, lions, or swans.

Turn the page to
find out which
came first.

Which Came First?

Washing Machine

Hundreds of different kinds of washing machines were available before the electric washing machine was invented. There was one big problem with them, though. They had to be cranked by hand.

▲ **This woman turns a crank to use a washing machine.**

Dryer

Before the dryer, there was the clothesline, which people still use today. Wet clothes are hung on the line to dry in the air. Clothespins keep shirts and pants from falling to the ground or blowing away.

◀ **Drying clothes on a clothesline took a long time. Today a dryer can dry your clothes in less than an hour.**

Answer: Washing Machine

The electric washing machine was introduced in Chicago in 1908. It used an electric motor to swish clothes around a tub filled with water.

The electric dryer came along a few years later, around 1915. It used an electric motor to tumble clothes inside a drum filled with hot air.

Before washing machines were invented, one way to clean clothes was to rub them against rocks at the side of a river. Another way was to boil them in water.

Which Came First?

Turn the page to find out which came first.

Electric Iron

More than 1,000 years ago, the **Vikings** used the weight and heat from hot stones to smooth out **fabrics**. Today we use an electric iron to do the same job. Sometimes a shot of steam helps, too.

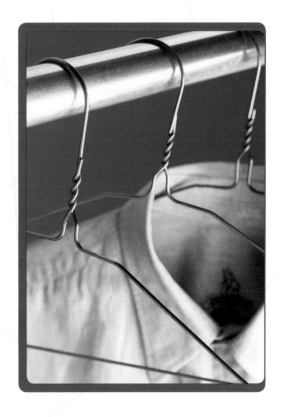

Wire Clothes Hanger

Thomas Jefferson invented the first wooden hanger. Yet it would be many years before the wire hanger we use today was created.

Answer: Electric Iron

The electric iron was invented in New York City. The year was 1882, and the inventor's name was Henry W. Seeley.

The wire hanger was invented in 1903 by Albert J. Parkhouse. He worked at a Michigan factory that made wire lampshade frames. One day, Parkhouse twisted some wire into a hanger because all the coat hooks in the factory were being used.

In a new sport called extreme ironing, **domestic daredevils** set down their ironing boards on tall cliffs, in harsh deserts, and even under water.

Turn the page to
find out which
came first.

Which Came First?

▲ **This dishwasher is about the size of a microwave oven.**

Dishwasher

At first, dishwashers were large and heavy. They were used mostly in hotels and restaurants. Later they became smaller, lighter, and less expensive. That's when they became popular for home use, too.

Vacuum Cleaner

To clean rugs, people used to hang them outside and beat them. It was hard work. Now they just turn on the vacuum cleaner—a truly neat invention!

◀ **Most vacuum cleaners need to be pushed to make them move. This one, however, zips around the room on its own.**

Answer: Dishwasher

In 1886 in Illinois, Josephine Cochrane invented the first successful dishwasher. Few homes had electricity then, so it was powered by hand. A few years later, she founded a company that would make electric dishwashers.

Hubert Cecil Booth, a Scottish **engineer**, made the first vacuum cleaner in 1901. It was so large that it had to be moved around on its own horse-drawn cart.

Josephine Cochrane decided to invent a dishwashing machine because she thought her servants were breaking too many of her expensive dishes!

▼ **Dishwasher from 1921**

Turn the page to
find out which
came first.

Which Came First?

Knife

A knife is a handy **eating utensil**. Yet during the **Middle Ages** a host did not set the table with knives because guests would bring their own.

◀ **Knives were often attached to belts that men wore.**

Fork

The parts that stick out of a fork are called *tines*. On today's forks, tines have points so that food can be speared. They are also usually curved so that food can be scooped up.

◀ **The first forks had only two tines. They were used to carve and serve meat.**

15

Answer: Knife

Knives have been around since **prehistoric** times. Hunters started making and using them more than 40,000 years ago. The first knives were made from sharp pieces of stone. Later, they were made out of metal.

Forks, on the other hand, have only been around for a few thousand years. They were first made and used in ancient Greece. However, they did not catch on as popular eating utensils in Europe until the 1600s.

In 1669, King Louis XIV of France banned sharp, pointed knives to cut down on knife fights. After the ban, knives with rounded ends became popular in France and throughout Europe.

Turn the page to find out which came first.

Which Came First?

Microwave Oven

A microwave oven cooks food much faster than a regular oven or stove does. In just six minutes, it can bake a potato. A regular oven takes about one hour.

Pop-up Toaster

People enjoyed making and eating toast long before the electric toaster was invented. How did they do it? They put a piece of bread on a toasting fork and held it over a fire.

◀ **An inside view of a pop-up toaster**

Answer: Pop-up Toaster

The pop-up toaster was invented in 1919 by Charles Strite. Toasters that didn't pop up the bread had already been around for ten years.

In 1945, an American scientist named Percy L. Spencer noticed that a certain piece of **radar** equipment could cook food. This discovery led to the "Radarange" two years later. It was the world's first microwave oven.

▲ Today, many pop-up toasters have wider openings. People can now toast not only bread slices but frozen waffles and bagels as well.

Toaster sales got a big boost around 1930. That's the time when packaged sliced bread first appeared.

Turn the page to
find out which
came first.

Which Came First?

Plastic Cling Wrap

There are hundreds of different kinds of plastics. Kitchen-wrap plastic is special because it is clear and clingy. These qualities also explain its number-one use—covering leftovers.

▲ When it comes to microwave cooking, it's fine to use plastic wrap. Never use aluminum foil, though—it might cause a fire.

Aluminum Foil

Aluminum foil is also good for saving leftovers. You can wrap it around just about any food or bend it into almost any shape.

◄ Unlike plastic wrap, aluminum foil can be used for baking in a regular oven.

19

Answer: Aluminum Foil

Aluminum foil was first sold for household use in 1947, two years after World War II ended. Aluminum had not been available for use in homes during the war because it was needed to make airplanes and submarines.

Plastic cling wrap was first marketed in 1953. The plastic used to make the wrap also played a role in the war. It was sprayed on planes to protect them from salty sea air.

Aluminum foil keeps food from sticking to the grill. This new use for foil helped spread the popularity of the backyard barbecue in the 1950s and 1960s.

Turn the page to
find out which
came first.

Which Came First?

Smoke Alarm

Smoke alarms save lives. **Statistics** show that deaths from fires have been reduced by half in homes that have them.

◀ **Safety experts recommend checking smoke-alarm batteries once a month and changing them at least once a year.**

Home Security System

Like smoke alarms, home **security** systems protect our safety and our property. How? If someone breaks into a home, the system sends a warning to people at the security company, who can then call the police.

Answer: Home Security System

The home security system got its start in Boston in 1858. Edwin T. Holmes began selling a bell with electric wiring. Known as the "**burglar** **alarm**," it could be set up in doors and windows to warn of break-ins.

The smoke alarm was invented in 1969 and quickly became an important safety tool. Today smoke alarms are found in almost every home.

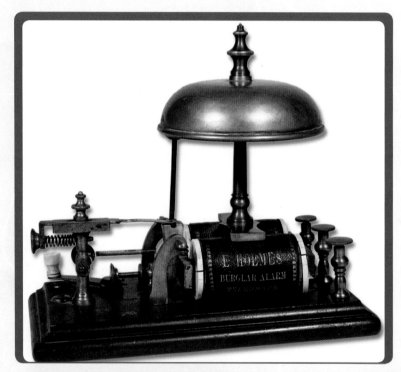

▲ **This is what Holmes's burglar alarm looked like in 1867.**

Holmes worked hard to sell his product. At one point, he built a special safe and offered prize money to anyone who could break into it without setting off the alarm.

Which Came First?

Alarm Clock

Alarm clocks are useful, but they're also unpopular. In a recent survey, Americans were asked what invention they hate the most but can't live without. Alarm clocks came in second, right after cell phones.

◀ **In the past, many clocks had to be wound by hand every day. Otherwise, they would stop running. Today many clocks run on batteries.**

Electric Lightbulb

Inside a lightbulb is a thin metal wire. When electricity flows through the wire, it gets so hot that it glows brightly and makes light.

New York lit up at night ▶

Answer: Alarm Clock

Clocks dating back to the 1500s had alarms, but those **timepieces** were large and heavy. Many had to be hung on walls. The first bedside alarm clock was invented in 1876.

A lightbulb for home use followed three years later, in 1879. It was the most famous invention to come out of the workshop of a great inventor—Thomas Alva Edison.

Since 1928, people have been able to wake up to music or news on the radio. That's the year that clock radios were first sold.

Which Comes Next?

Here are two new possibilities for the home that inventors have come up with. Which one do you think will catch on?

The Spork

Originally invented for the U.S. Armed Forces, this eating utensil has also been used in schools, prisons, and fast-food restaurants. As its name suggests, it is a combination of a spoon and a fork.

The Clocky

This alarm clock on wheels doesn't just ring. It also rolls off your nightstand and hides. If you want to turn it off, you have to find it first. Now, who could sleep through that?

Scorecard

How many did you get correct?

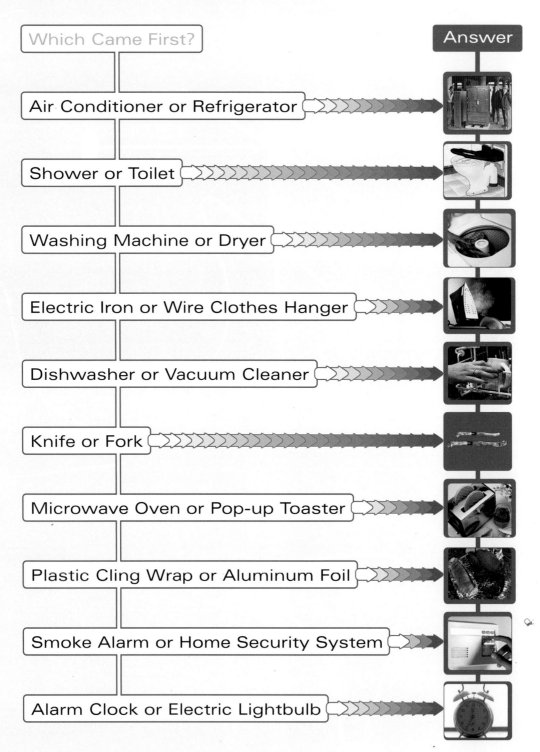

Which Came First?	Answer
Air Conditioner or Refrigerator	
Shower or Toilet	
Washing Machine or Dryer	
Electric Iron or Wire Clothes Hanger	
Dishwasher or Vacuum Cleaner	
Knife or Fork	
Microwave Oven or Pop-up Toaster	
Plastic Cling Wrap or Aluminum Foil	
Smoke Alarm or Home Security System	
Alarm Clock or Electric Lightbulb	

Bonus Questions

Now you know which of the household inventions in this book came first. Here are a few bonus questions.

1. **Which invention costs the most to run in a year of normal use?**

   a. washing machine
   b. dryer
   c. refrigerator
   d. microwave oven

2. **How much did the first electric iron weigh?**

   a. 2 pounds (1 kg)
   b. 5 pounds (2 kg)
   c. 10 pounds (5 kg)
   d. 15 pounds (7 kg)

3. **Which invention sold well early on because people knew it would help rid their homes of germs?**

   a. the air conditioner
   b. the vacuum cleaner
   c. aluminum foil
   d. the pop-up toaster

4. **Percy L. Spencer discovered that radar equipment could cook food when it accidentally melted which item in his pocket?**

   a. a plastic pen
   b. a dime
   c. a stick of gum
   d. a candy bar

Answers: 1. c; 2. d; 3. b; 4. d

Just the Facts

✻ At the first Thanksgiving in 1621, the Pilgrims used knives and spoons, but they did not use forks. Forks would not be widely used in Massachusetts for another 200 years or so.

✻ In 1596, Sir John Harrington designed and built a flushing toilet for his godmother, Queen Elizabeth I of England. People laughed at his invention, though, and it would take almost 200 years for toilets to be made again in England.

✻ In 1902, an English inventor made an early version of a fire alarm. The alarm sounded when the temperature went high enough to melt a block of butter within the device.

✻ A new kind of smoke detector can be programmed to call a child's name. Why? Children sleep more deeply than adults. They are more likely to wake up to the sound of their names than to a regular alarm.

✻ More than 3,000 years ago, the ancient Egyptians made clay pots with small holes that worked as water clocks. Marks inside the pots told what time it was as the water drained out. Later, the ancient Greeks invented a water alarm clock. When the water reached a certain point, it made a mechanical bird whistle.

The History of Household Inventions

**Prehistoric Times
(more than 40,000 years ago)**
Hunters made knives

1600s Forks widely used in Europe

1775 Modern toilet begins to be
developed in England

1858 Home security system
(burglar alarm) first sold

1876 Bedside alarm clock invented

1879 Edison's electric
lightbulb invented

1882 Electric iron invented

1886 Dishwasher invented

Early 1900s Bathtubs with built-in
showers first sold

1901 First vacuum cleaner

1903 Wire clothes hanger invented

1908 Electric washing machine introduced

1913–1927 Modern refrigerator developed

About 1915 Electric dryer invented

1919 Pop-up toaster invented

1929 Household air conditioners first sold

1945–1947 Microwave oven developed

1947 Aluminum foil first sold for home use

1953 Plastic cling wrap first sold

1969 Smoke alarm invented

Glossary

appliances (uh-PLYE-uhnss-uhz)   machines that do specific jobs, such as cleaning or cooling

burglar (BURG-lur)   a person who breaks into a building and steals things; a thief

daredevils (DAIR-*dev*-ilz)   people who do dangerous or risky things

domestic (duh-MESS-tik)   having to do with the home

eating utensil (EET-ing yoo-TEN-suhl)   a tool used for eating

engineer (en-juh-NIHR)   a person who designs and builds things, such as machines, bridges, vehicles, and roads

fabrics (FAB-riks)   cloth

imported (im-PORT-id)   brought from another country

Middle Ages (MID-uhl AYJ-iz)   the period of European history from about the 400s to around 1500

plumbing (PLUHM-ing)   the pipes and other equipment that carry water into and out of a building

prehistoric (*pree*-hi-STOR-ik)   more than 5,500 years ago, which is before the time people began to use writing to record history

radar (RAY-dar)   a device that uses radio waves to locate objects such as planes and ships

security (si-KYOOR-ih-tee)   safety

statistics (stuh-TISS-tiks)   information in the form of numbers

timepieces (TIME-*peess*-iz)   objects, such as clocks or watches, that measure time

Vikings (VYE-kings)   a group of warriors who lived from the late 700s to about 1100 in the area that is now Denmark, Norway, and Sweden

Bibliography

Panati, Charles. *Panati's Extraordinary Origins of Everyday Things*. New York: HarperCollins (1989).

Strasser, Susan. *Never Done: A History of American Housework*. New York: Pantheon Books (1982).

Weaver, Rebecca, and Rodney Dale. *Machines in the Home*. New York: Oxford University Press (1993).

Read More

Alphin, Elaine Marie. *Irons*. Minneapolis, MN: Carolrhoda Books (1998).

Alphin, Elaine Marie. *Toasters*. Minneapolis, MN: Carolrhoda Books (1998).

Alphin, Elaine Marie. *Vacuum Cleaners*. Minneapolis, MN: Carolrhoda Books (1997).

Platt, Richard. *Smithsonian Visual Timeline of Inventions*. New York: DK Publishing (2001).

Rubin, Susan Goldman. *Toilets, Toasters, and Telephones: The How and Why of Everyday Objects*. San Diego, CA: Browndeer Press/Harcourt Brace & Company (1998).

Learn More Online

Visit these Web sites to learn more about household inventions:

http://inventors.about.com/library/bl/bl12.htm

www.historychannel.com/exhibits/hometech/index.html

Index

About the Author

Natalie Lunis is the author of more than two dozen science books for children. She keeps her household in the New York City area.